WORLD ISSUES

GENETIC REVOLUTION

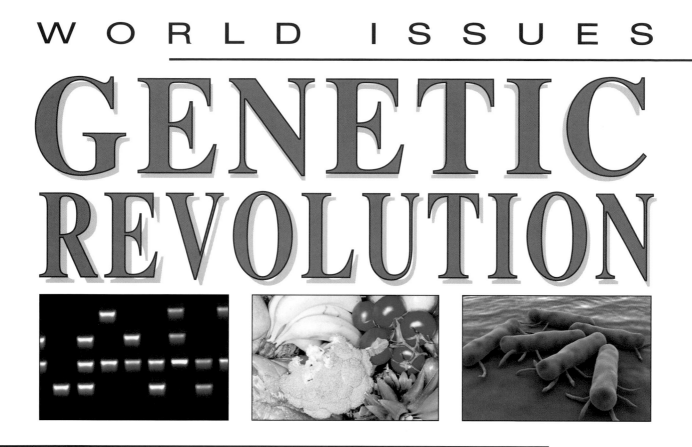

A look at the way the world is today

Ewan McLeish

Franklin Watts
London • Sydney

ABOUT THIS BOOK

Since the discovery of the genetic code in the 1950s, scientists have begun to unlock the secrets of life. Today, we know the genetic code for the entire human body. We can take genetic information from one creature and put it into another. We even have the power to create exact copies of ourselves. This book explores this genetic revolution, how it works and the effects it may have on life on Earth. We also take a closer look at the responsibilities that accompany these amazing discoveries.

© Aladdin Books Ltd 2006
Produced by
Aladdin Books Ltd
2/3 Fitzroy Mews
London W1T 6DF

ISBN 0–7496–6268–9

First published in 2006 by

Franklin Watts	Franklin Watts Australia
338 Euston Road	Hachette Children's Books
London	Level 17/207 Kent Street
NW1 3BH	Sydney NSW 2000

Designer: Flick, Book Design and Graphics
Editor: Harriet Brown
Picture Researcher: Alexa Brown

The author, Dr Ewan McLeish, is a writer and lecturer in education. He has written over 20 books on science and the environment.

The consultant, Dr Jon Turney, is a senior visiting fellow in the Department of Science and Technology Studies, University College London, and a visiting lecturer in the Science Communication Group at Imperial College, London.

Printed in Malaysia

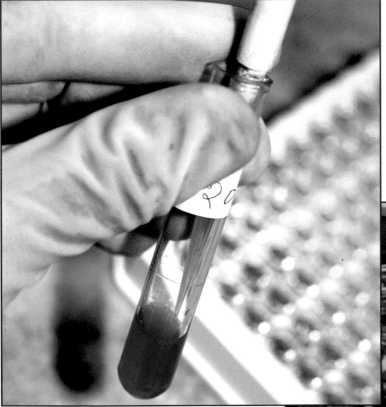

CONTENTS

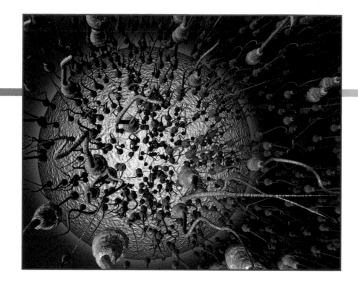

INTRODUCTION

Have you ever wondered how we come to look the way we do? Or have you ever thought why a bean seed grows into a particular kind of plant and not another kind? The answer lies in genes. The cells from which almost all organisms are made contain a chemical genetic code that dictates how they will develop. The code dictates your hair colour or the shape of a bean leaf. Today, we are learning more and more about the genetic code and, just as importantly, how it can be changed. Changing the genetic code is called genetic engineering. Some people think that genetic engineering is wrong and could even threaten life on Earth. Others believe it could have a positive impact on our world. This book may help you make up your mind.

Boy in a bubble

Richard has spent his whole life in a plastic bubble, and without the bubble he will die. It protects him from thousands of different infections that other children's bodies normally fight and destroy. Richard has no such defences because he has a medical condition called Severe Combined Immunity Deficiency (SCID). He has this condition because of a problem with his genetic code. The condition means that his body has no natural protection against disease. Until a cure is fully developed, the best way to keep him alive is to keep the bacteria and viruses that can kill him from coming into contact with him. This is why he lives in a bubble.

Cotton capers

In much of southern India, cotton is life. It is the main crop in this region, and the market for cotton is huge. The world needs clothes, and cotton provides the raw material for many of them. The sale of cotton abroad brings in much-needed income for people here. However, there is a problem. Bollworms are small caterpillars which eat the cotton heads (bolls). This means that the cotton plants produce less cotton. The caterpillars can be killed by chemical sprays called pesticides. But the sprays are poisons that kill other organisms too, and sometimes get washed into rivers and streams. In addition, the bollworms are becoming resistant to the spray and it is becoming less and less effective.

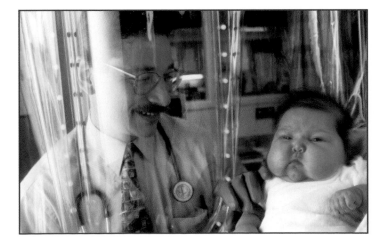

Bollworms destroy cotton plants. Changing the genetic code of the plant so it is resistant to the pest may offer a solution.

Two problems – one solution?

Two very different problems, but both are matters of life and death. They may have a common solution. The answer may be to alter the genetic codes that cause the problems in the first place. If Richard's genes were changed, he might develop the healthy white blood cells he needs to fight infection. Then he would no longer have to live in a bubble.

In India, the genetic codes of the cotton plants are being changed – different genes have been added to the plants. This helps the plants to become more resistant to the effects of the bollworm. In some regions, cotton yields are already up by 80 per cent.

The beginning of a revolution

We now have the power to take genes from one organism and put them into another. We can take a gene from a cold-water fish and put it into a strawberry plant so it continues to grow in the cold. We can make the life-giving drug insulin by putting a human gene into bacteria that turns them into tiny insulin factories. We have the power to make exact copies of farm animals and, although it has not yet been done, even ourselves. It is a genetic revolution.

The power of life

The genetic revolution may also bring dangers. This new technology is very powerful, and we do not yet know what some of the effects may be – either on ourselves or on the world in which we live. Once we insert different genes into living things, it may be hard to remove them again. Some people think we cannot afford to ignore all the possibilities that our new knowledge opens up. Others think we should stop and think hard before we rush into the new genetic age.

SOME HELPFUL TERMS

Bases – The parts of the DNA molecule which determine the genetic code.

Cells – The tiny building blocks from which all organisms are made.

Chromosome – A long strand of DNA.

DNA – A molecule in the shape of a spiral staircase. The 'steps' of the staircase are made up of chemicals known as 'bases'. There are four types of bases, and the way in which the numerous bases are arranged creates the genetic code. DNA is found inside cells.

Gene – A short section of DNA. Genes are a specific arrangement of 'bases'. Genes tell the body how to develop and determine which characteristics are passed on to the next generation.

Genetic code – The set of instructions that determines the growth, type, shape and other characteristics of a living organism. The genetic code is formed by the arrangement of the 'bases'.

Genetic engineering – The alteration of the genetic code of an organism.

GM – Genetic modification, or genetically modified.

5

GENES 'R' US

In the middle of the 20th century, scientists were on the brink of an important discovery. They were about to reveal the exact structure of a substance in cells they knew to be at the heart of the genetic code. The substance was DNA. But perhaps even they could not have predicted where this discovery would lead.

DNA revealed

Two scientists in particular were about to make the breakthrough and decipher the most important code in the world. Their discovery would help explain how each animal and plant comes to look the way it does and, perhaps even more importantly, how it passes on this information to the next generation. In 1953, the scientists were studying a substance (or molecule) called DNA, found in the nucleus of cells. They knew that DNA played a vital role in deciding and passing on features such as height or hair and eye colour. After months of study, they finally worked out the actual shape of the DNA molecule. It was a spiral made of two long strands, joined by shorter cross-strands, like a twisted rope ladder or spiral staircase. This was to become known as the famous double helix!

Crick and Watson

The scientists were a Briton, Francis Crick, and an American, James Watson. Almost overnight, they became the most famous scientists in the world. Later, in 1962, they were awarded the Nobel Prize, along with their New Zealander colleague, Maurice

James Watson and Francis Crick discovered the double helix shape of DNA. This unlocked the sequence of the genetic code.

Wilkins, for their fantastic discovery. A fourth scientist, British-born Rosalind Franklin, may also have received the Nobel Prize for her contributions to the discovery, but she died in 1958. Working out the shape of DNA was the first step to understanding how features or characteristics are passed down through generations. DNA holds all the information necessary to shape life and once the structure of DNA was known, Watson and Crick had paved the way for a genetic revolution that would change the world.

DNA – The stuff of life

Organisms are made from tiny cells. Cells form our tissues and organs. At the centre of a cell is the nucleus. This is the control centre of the cell. Inside the nucleus there are a number of X-shaped structures called chromosomes. Different organisms have different numbers of chromosomes. Humans have 46 per cell and tomatoes have 24. Half of the chromosomes come from the father and half come from the mother. So, you have two copies of each chromosome – one from each parent.

Chromosomes are made of tightly coiled DNA. If you could uncoil the DNA in one human cell it would be around two metres long. Because humans are made of billions of cells, the DNA of the whole human body would be over a hundred billion kilometres long!

On each chromosome there are many many genes, which are segments of DNA. The DNA forms a code which is responsible for making proteins – the building blocks of our bodies. As you can see, DNA really is the stuff of life.

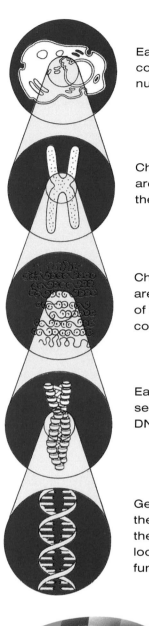

Each cell contains a nucleus.

Chromosomes are found inside the nucleus.

Chromosomes are packages of tightly coiled DNA.

Each gene is a section of the DNA spiral.

Genes describe the formation of the body, how it looks and how it functions.

7

Each rung of the 'ladder' is made from two chemicals called bases. The arrangement of the bases forms a code.

In this diagram, each different colour – green, blue, pink and orange – is a different base. There are only four bases in total.

Chromosome

All about genes

Watson and Crick's brilliant discovery was that genes are actually segments of the DNA molecule. As you can see from the previous illustration, the DNA ladder's 'rungs' are made from chemicals called 'bases'. These are quite simple substances and there are only four different types. They are arranged in groups of three, rather like three-letter words. The order in which they are arranged on the DNA strand forms the code. In this way, an almost infinite number of sentences or messages can be created. Each different message is a different gene.

Proteins = life

Each gene tells the cell to produce a particular type of molecule on which all life is based – a protein. We all need proteins to grow and develop, but proteins are not just what makes our muscles strong. In order for our bodies to function properly, thousands of chemical reactions are constantly taking place in our cells. None of these reactions can take place without proteins being present.

The body builds these proteins from smaller building blocks called amino acids. Genes tell the cell how to put these building blocks together in order to make the proteins our bodies need. Genes really are us!

When genes go wrong

Unfortunately, genes do not always work perfectly. Sometimes a fault (a mutation) develops in the code and a particular gene goes wrong. It no longer produces the protein it is supposed to build. One protein out of thousands may not sound that serious. Sometimes it isn't, but sometimes the result is a crippling illness like motor neurone disease or cystic fibrosis. Most of the time, our genes serve us well. When they malfunction, however, we may be in trouble.

Genetic modification

In 1983, exactly 30 years after the structure of DNA was discovered, and after many years of

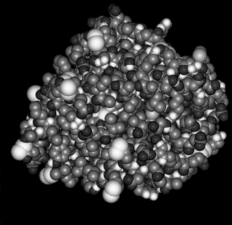

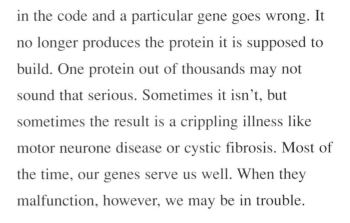

Proteins are large, three-dimensional molecules. Genes tell the body which proteins to create. This is a model of a protein molecule.

8

painstaking research, a team of American scientists made another breakthrough. They managed to transfer a gene from a microscopic organism, called a bacterium, into a tobacco plant (tobacco plants are easy to grow and work with). It was the first time a plant had been successfully 'genetically modified'.

Now, almost another 25 years on, most of us are familiar with the term genetic modification (GM), or genetic engineering. We hear it on the news and read about it in newspapers and magazines. If we look at the ingredients lists on packets of food, we may find it mentioned. We may also find claims that a product is 'GM-free'. As we shall see, the subject of genetic modification is one that raises strong emotions, both for and against.

Our ability to change the genetic codes of different plants and animals goes far beyond the contents of a supermarket trolley. Few areas of our lives are

Much debate surrounds the growth and consumption of genetically modified crops.

untouched by the genetic revolution. From medicine to manufacturing, from farming to forensics, it plays an important role. Imagine you can remove faulty genes and replace them with ones that work. Imagine that you can add useful genes from other plants, animals and bacteria. This is the power to change life.

As we shall see in the next chapter, there are many ways of transferring genes from one organism to another. We now have the technology to change or modify the genetic make-up of almost any living organism, and that includes ourselves. However we may describe it, it is truly a genetic revolution.

9

Tobacco was one of the first plants to be genetically modified.

TRANSFERRING GENES

Moving genes from one organism to another is not a simple process. Often it ends in failure rather than success. Some of the methods used may seem surprising. For example, in plants, a gene can be literally shot into a cell on a tiny particle of metal. In both plants and animals, genes are often transferred using a 'carrier' such as a bacterium or virus. One group of people who have benefited from this type of gene transfer are those suffering from diabetes.

Many diabetics must have insulin injections each day. Genetically modified bacteria can ensure we have an unlimited supply of this life-saving drug.

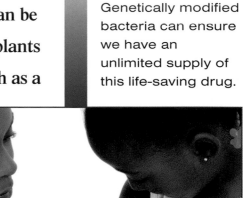

What is diabetes?

Close to the small intestine is a large organ called the pancreas. In healthy people, the pancreas produces insulin. Insulin converts glucose in the blood into a form in which it can be stored in the liver and muscles. In diabetics, the pancreas does not work properly. Without enough insulin, their blood glucose levels rise. If this continues unchecked, the patient can go into a coma and eventually die. In most diabetes sufferers, the worst effects of the disease can be controlled by taking insulin at regular intervals, either orally (by mouth)

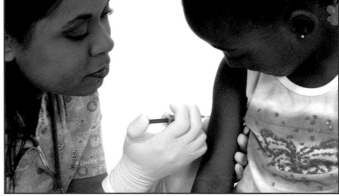

or, more commonly, by injection. Properly treated, diabetes is no barrier to achievement. Sir Steve Redgrave, the famous Olympic rower, is a sufferer, as are many other successful and active people.

Where to find insulin?

In the past, insulin could not be obtained in large or pure enough quantities to meet the growing need for the drug. Supplies normally came from other animals, mainly pigs and cows. Concerns, such as the BSE scare ('mad cow disease') in 1986, meant that alternative sources were needed. What was required was a large supply of insulin that could be produced quickly and to the same high quality every time.

Supplies of insulin used to come from pigs or cows. Scares about animal health encouraged the search for ways to produce pure insulin artificially.

Bacteria to the rescue

The answer came in the form of a bacterium called *Escherichia coli* (*E. coli* for short). This is a common bacterium found almost everywhere. Scientists knew a lot about it and, as it was easy to grow in a laboratory, it was the ideal candidate! Suppose the gene that causes insulin production in humans could somehow be inserted into the genetic code of the bacteria. Could it then be tricked into producing insulin suitable for human use? The answer was, it could, but only after years of painstaking research and many failed attempts. Now insulin is produced routinely all over the world in this way. Shortage of supply and risk of infection is unlikely to be a problem again.

Getting plasmids to do the work

Unlike animal or plant cells, bacterial cells do not have a nucleus. The chromosomes are packed 'loose' within the cell itself. They also have extra genetic material, called plasmids. A plasmid is a tiny circular piece of DNA. Plasmids can be taken out of a bacterium. New bits of DNA can be added to a plasmid, which is then re-inserted into a bacterium.

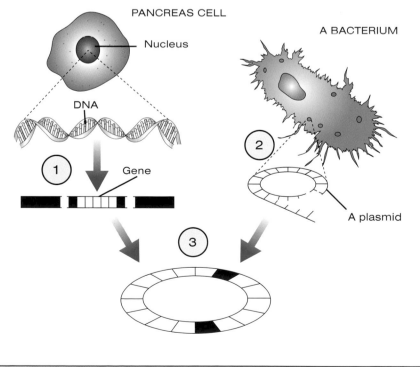

E. coli is a common bacteria that is extremely useful in scientific research.

How is this done?

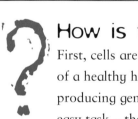

First, cells are removed from the pancreas of a healthy human. Finding the insulin-producing gene they contain is not an easy task – there are nearly 25,000 genes in humans. Special chemicals, called enzymes, make it possible.

(1) Chemicals which recognise the gene are used to cut it out from the DNA of a human pancreas cell.

(2) The same chemicals are used to cut open a circular piece of bacterial DNA (the plasmid). This creates a 'gap' into which the insulin gene fits exactly.

(3) The insulin-producing gene is inserted into the plasmid. Other chemicals are used to seal the join. The plasmid is finally returned to the bacterium which now contains the human insulin gene.

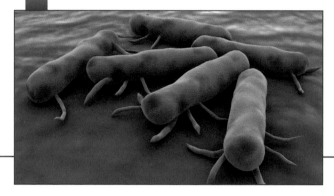

PANCREAS CELL

Nucleus

DNA

Gene

A BACTERIUM

A plasmid

The bacterium now carries the insulin-producing gene. Bacteria reproduce by dividing repeatedly – one bacterium divides in two, those two bacteria each divide in two, and so on. Eventually, there are millions of exact copies of the original bacterium. Each of these genetically modified bacteria will now be capable of producing human insulin, which can be collected and given to diabetes sufferers.

Target practice

Using plasmids is not the only way of putting a new gene into another organism. In genetically modified plants, genes can literally be shot into the cell's nucleus by attaching them to tiny particles of gold or tungsten metal.

In animals, it is common to use a genetically modified virus to deliver the genetic cargo. You will be familiar with viruses as tiny microscopic organisms capable of causing diseases such as measles or the common cold. They are not technically living things, but packages of DNA wrapped up in a protein coat.

Viruses can invade cells. Once inside, they can combine their own DNA with that of the animal they have invaded, called their 'host'. The virus makes the animal cell produce thousands of copies of the virus. Eventually, there are so many viruses in the cell that they break out. The escaped viruses go on to infect other cells, which often results in the host experiencing symptoms of a disease.

Safety first

The ability of viruses to combine their own DNA with the host cell's DNA makes them ideal as carriers. Genes can be inserted into the virus and the modified virus is then put into the host. The problem is that viruses can be pretty nasty things – they cause disease and few medicines are effective against them. To make them less dangerous, the virus is first deactivated so it can still invade cells but can no longer divide and create more copies of itself.

The use of viruses in genetic modification is not easy and does carry risks, as we will see later. Fortunately, other mechanisms are also available. For example, tiny structures found inside cells, called liposomes, can also do the job. Liposomes are minute oil-like droplets which can merge with the

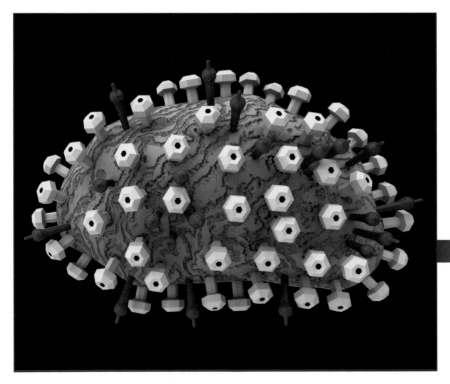

Viruses can be used to transfer genes into an organism. Their ability to combine their DNA with a cell's DNA enables them to do this.

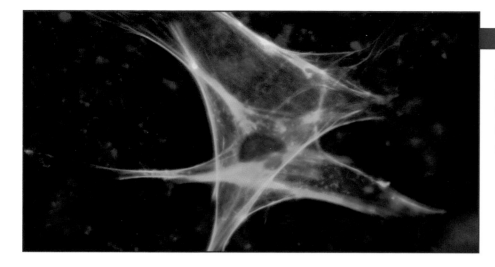

Liposomes fuse with the cell membrane that surrounds the cell. The green edge of this nerve cell is the cell membrane.

membrane (thin layer) that surrounds all animal cells. In this way, they can carry genes into the cell.

But getting a gene into a cell is only the beginning. To be successful, the gene has to work properly, that is, to produce the desired effect in the target cell. This is often not the case. Perhaps even more importantly, it is vital there are no ill effects that result from inserting the gene. This is especially true when we come to dealing with genetic modification in humans – what is known as gene therapy (see pages 27-31).

Nothing new?

In many senses, we have used what is now called biotechnology for thousands of years. For example, plants and animals have always been specially bred to improve particular features (or traits) such as disease resistance, size or hardiness. The making of bread, wine and beer uses a microscopic fungus called yeast. Even as far back as Roman times, people used bacterial 'leaching' to remove copper from natural deposits, a practice which still continues today. In this method, bacteria change the chemicals surrounding the copper, which extracts, or leaches, the copper metal from the natural deposits. This is an environmentally-friendly way of extracting copper because the bacteria already grow naturally in the copper mine.

But it was the discovery of the genetic code by Watson and Crick in 1953, and the later discovery of enzymes that could cut open and rejoin strands of DNA, that allowed us to actually move genes from one organism to another. Now, genetic modification is part of our daily lives, even if many people are unaware of it.

13

Doing it the Roman way

It is estimated that over 90 per cent of the copper mined worldwide is 'biomined'. The largest copper mine using bacteria for this purpose is the Quebrada Blanca in Chile. It processes 17,000 tonnes of ore per day and produces 75,000 tonnes of high-grade copper per year.

These massive reels of copper wire will be made into electric wires.

GM Crops – Modified or Mystified?

One of the most publicised uses of genetic engineering is genetically modified (GM) food. People wonder whether we need GM food, whether it is dangerous to eat and whether it is dangerous to the environment. However, others think that it is a vital way of providing the global population with enough food. Here we look at some of the facts and myths surrounding GM food; then you can make up your own mind.

There has been much talk about GM 'Frankenstein foods', such as giant or strangely-shaped fruits and vegetables. Proper debate is more helpful than scare stories.

What's in a name?

The term 'genetically modified' can mean many different things. As you can see from the box on the opposite page, there may not even be any trace of the original GM material in the food itself, since it has been lost during processing.

Enter the unsquashable tomato

The first GM food to be produced commercially appeared in American supermarkets in 1994. It was a tomato, genetically modified to stay firmer longer. This meant that the product was easier to transport and had a longer shelf life. Two years later, a type of GM tomato puree (crushed tomatoes) was available to buy in UK stores. Since that time, many different GM products have made their way onto our plates. They include genetically modified maize, oil seed rape (canola) and soya.

Benefits of GM crops

Crops are modified in a number of ways. By changing a crop's genetic code, it can be made resistant to herbicides or pesticides (so that only weeds and pests are attacked and not the GM crop), resistant to attack by viruses and other diseases, and made more hardy so that it will grow in poor soil or other unfavourable conditions. Crops can even be modified so that they provide extra nutrients and vitamins. GM crops may bring benefits to farmers and consumers all over the world and may be of particular use in parts of the developing world where food is scarce. Across the globe, in particular in the USA, Argentina, Canada and China, hundreds of thousands of square kilometres are used for growing GM crops.

GM Crops – Modified or Mystified?

The instant guide to GM food

GM food – Food coming directly from a crop or animal that has been genetically modified.

GM ingredients – Food containing a GM product, such as GM maize flour.

GM processing aid – Food in which a GM organism (for example, a bacterium) has been used to produce a product (such as an enzyme) to help in the manufacturing process, such as cheese making.

GM derived ingredients – Food that comes from a GM crop but no longer contains GM DNA, for example, soy oil.

GM ingredients in animal feed – Refers to the meat that comes from animals fed on GM crops.

There is no evidence that eating foods containing altered genes can make you ill. Some people are still concerned about possible long-term effects, however.

Despite the many possible benefits, many people were, and still are, very suspicious of GM products. So what's all the fuss about?

Is GM food safe to eat?

People have two main concerns. The first – is GM food safe to eat? The idea of 'foreign' genes being inserted into plants or animals worries many people. Could these genes damage people's health? Some food plants have been modified to make them more resistant to pests – to carry their own in-built 'pesticides'. Some wonder whether these can harm people as well as insects.

Others are concerned about what is known as 'antibiotic resistance'. When genes are inserted into bacteria, antibiotics are sometimes used to find and select the cells that have successfully taken up the added gene. If the antibiotic kills a cell, it hasn't taken up the gene. So, the remaining cells that have taken up the gene are antibiotic-resistant. Could these antibiotic-resistant cells pass on their resistance to people, making them immune to vital medicines? People even talk about 'Frankenstein foods', conjuring up images of strange deformed crops lurking in our fields!

Exaggerated concerns

Others feel the concerns are greatly exaggerated. After all, they argue, genes themselves are not harmful to eat and they are quickly digested. All food products are tested before being sold and this includes checking for the presence of possible harmful products.

At present, there is little evidence to suggest eating genetically modified foods can be harmful. The question of antibiotic resistance is more difficult, however. There is some evidence that gut bacteria – naturally occurring, harmless bacteria in the digestive system – can take up antibiotic resistance from GM products. But there is no evidence that this can be transferred to other cells in the body, or to other, harmful organisms.

The case of the genetically modified soya

In April 2003, a toxic cloud arrived in Colonia Loma Senés, in northern Argentina. The poison blew onto plots of land and into houses. It made the villagers' eyes sting and the children's bare legs developed bad rashes. Almost all of the crops were badly damaged and over the next few days and weeks chickens and pigs died, and goats gave birth to dead or deformed young. Months later, banana trees still did not bear edible fruit.

The villagers were quick to blame neighbouring farmers who were growing genetically modified soya.

What had happened?

The soya was genetically modified so that it was resistant to a very powerful herbicide called glyphosphate. When the herbicide was used, it was meant to kill all the weeds and not the soya. At first, the results were very promising. The new soya variety grew well and the farmers only needed to spray their crops with the glyphosphate herbicide once or twice a year.

Soon, nearly half of all agricultural land was used for soya beans, grown to meet the huge market for cattle feed around the world. Then, gradually, things started to go wrong. The farmers found they had to spray more often as the weeds became more resistant to the glyphosphate herbicide. By 2003, ten times more weedkiller was being used than in 1997.

Herbicide spraying increased massively in Argentina, possibly as a result of growing GM soya (see photo below left).

At the same time, beneficial soil bacteria began to decline and the soil became less fertile. Yields began to fall.

Gain or blame?

Some blamed the herbicide, and therefore the GM soya. Others thought that the soil fertility had declined because only one crop was being grown and the nutrients were constantly being taken out of the soil by the soya. Whichever the real reason, over 150,000 small farmers were driven from the land because of the poor soil, and the production of 'staples' like milk, rice, maize, potatoes and lentils fell sharply. One local scientist said:

"The country has adopted GM technology more rapidly than any other country in the world. It didn't take proper safeguards to manage resistance and to protect the fertility of its soils. This cannot be sustained."

Perhaps if the growing of the new GM soya had been managed more closely, there would not have been such problems.

People blamed the GM soya for their problems because they had to use a powerful herbicide they might not have used with normal plants.

16

Do GM crops harm the environment?

Even if GM crops are safe to eat, there are other concerns. Genetically modifying plants to be resistant to a single, powerful herbicide should mean less herbicide overall has to be used. As we have already seen, this is not always the case. Another question is – would crops genetically modified to be resistant to insect pests harm beneficial insects, too? And what would happen to the animals and birds that depended on them? Then, there is the question of contamination. Suppose genes inserted into crop plants somehow 'escaped' and got into wild plants or weeds. We might be creating 'super-weeds' that would be resistant to the very herbicides that were designed to protect the crops.

Once again, the evidence is far from clear. In a 'farm trial', carried out in the UK between 1999 and 2003, scientists found that fields containing GM oil seed rape and sugar beet contained fewer bees and butterflies than conventionally grown (normal) crops. This was because there were fewer weeds to provide food and cover. There were also fewer weed seeds, which are important for birds as a source of food. On the other hand, GM maize seemed to be better for wildlife than normal maize.

In addition, a recent study showed that the worldwide growth of GM crops is helping to reduce greenhouse gas emissions from agricultural practices. Practices such as ploughing and tilling use large amounts of fuel. Some GM crops need less ploughing and tilling than normal crops and, in this way, farmers can reduce their greenhouse gas emissions.

Some GM crops seem to be good for wildlife, whereas in other cases, GM crops seem to cause a reduction in wildlife numbers.

Some people campaign against GM food products. However, others support genetic engineering as a way of increasing food production.

More research needed?

The trials of GM crops are intended to allow scientists to find out the effects that the crops have on the environment. However, they have caused many arguments. Some people think that the trials are meaningless because they do not look at the possible effects on soil fertility, or at the possibility of contamination of other crops or wild plants by GM seeds or pollen. Such contamination has been shown to occur in a number of countries. For example, pollen from GM grass has been found to pollinate non-GM grass over 20 km away, and GM seeds can be carried by the wind for up to 8 km. The difficulty comes in deciding whether the benefits of GM crops, such as providing enough food for people, reducing the use of chemicals on crops and reducing greenhouse gas emissions, outweigh the dangers.

Animal farm

So far we have looked mainly at genetically modified crops. What about animals that are farmed? Research is underway to create cows that produce more protein in their milk and sheep with softer wool. In some Mediterranean countries, scientists are looking at ways of introducing genes to make insect pests sterile (unable to reproduce) or pass on a gene that kills their offspring. In Japan, a scientist has even created pigs implanted with a spinach gene. The gene is believed to convert saturated fat into unsaturated fat, making it healthier to eat. Other scientists have modified a growth hormone (a chemical that controls growth rate) gene in salmon by adding another gene that is not affected by temperature. This allows the fish to go on growing, even in cold winter waters.

Right or wrong?

How do you feel about some of these developments? Many of the issues we looked at in plants also apply to animals. But there are other considerations. Unlike plants, animals are what we call sentient creatures – they are aware of what is going on around them. They feel pain or discomfort. We have to treat them with dignity and consideration. Of course, that applies to animals in general, not just those that are genetically modified.

Some people think that genetically modifying animals, purely for our benefit, is morally wrong and should be banned. Others say it is no more than we have been doing, in other ways, for thousands of years. Animals are bred to have certain characteristics (such as high milk production) by repeatedly mating only those individuals with the desired feature. Eventually, the gene for high milk production becomes established in all the offspring. We call this selective breeding. How is this any different to modifying an animal's genes in a laboratory? As long as the animals are not harmed in any way, some argue that it is not wrong to improve them by genetic modification.

In the name of the law?

In European countries, it is legal to grow or import GM food as long as the risks to the environment and health are carefully assessed (examined), the public is consulted and the EU (European Union) approves. In the case of animals, other regulations concerning animal rearing and welfare also apply.

In theory, therefore, there is nothing to prevent a European country, such as Britain, from growing GM crops, for example. In fact, very few companies seem willing to take the risk of doing this commercially. For one thing, restrictions on keeping GM crops separated from conventional crops are quite strict. For another, the market for GM products is limited. As we have already seen, the general public is still suspicious of the technology and in general is not aware of the benefits.

On the other hand, there are plenty of GM products imported into Europe, including the UK. Many of these come from the United States and Canada where suspicion about GM crops is much lower, and production much higher. As we have also seen, countries like Argentina grow millions of tonnes of soya every year, much of which ends up as cattle feed. People in the UK may then eat the GM-soya-fed cattle.

A large amount of cattle feed is made using soya. Much of this is now genetically modified, although this is unlikely to be a health risk either for people or cattle.

19

In some countries, food labels tell you whether the product contains any GM foods. However, the rules governing GM product labelling are less strict in the USA and Canada, than in Europe.

What's in your shopping basket?

Although eating GM foods does not seem to cause harm to health, some people still have their doubts. In many European countries, well-known supermarket chains have decided to ban GM ingredients in their own brand range. However, they cannot guarantee that meat is reared on a GM-free diet (unless it is organically grown).

This is where labelling comes in. In April 2004, new EU rules were agreed, designed to give customers more information about GM food. This includes labelling all foods containing GM ingredients or produced from GM crops. In other parts of the world, such as China, Thailand and Sri Lanka, similar rules governing labelling have also been put in place.

Problems with labelling

Foods contain many different ingredients and tracking all of them is not easy. People argue that many foods are excluded from labelling. These include food made with the help of GM technology (such as some cheeses produced with GM bacteria) and meat or milk products from animals raised on GM feed.

Attitudes to GM food and labelling vary across the world. In the USA, for example, GM foods are widely available and accepted by the public. As a result, labelling of GM foods in the USA is voluntary.

In most countries, all foods that reach the supermarket shelves must be safe for human consumption, whether or not they contain GM ingredients.

FEED THE WORLD?

Many people all over the world suffer because they do not have enough food to eat. Some parts of the world have poor soil or too little rainfall, which prevents the people from growing enough crops for food. Some people think that genetic engineering can solve some of the world's food shortages by creating crops that can thrive in harsh conditions. In addition, crops can be modified to contain more vitamins and iron to combat the effects of poor diet.

Tough plants

In 2004, a group of scientists launched some revolutionary plants. Using genetic engineering, the scientists had created tomato and rice plants that would grow in soils rich in salt. They were even able to survive conditions of extreme cold and drought. These plants had been created in a slightly different way than before. Rather than adding genes from other plants, they had increased the plants' natural defences by amplifying (increasing) some of their own genes.

One of these genes makes a plant pump salt out of its roots before the salt can do too much damage. In many poorer parts of the world, large areas of agricultural land are lost because the soil contains so much salt. This happens when salt deposits, which usually lie deep beneath the soil, are brought to the surface by poor irrigation (watering) methods. If crops can be made to grow in salt-rich soil, vast areas that are so arid and infertile that they have practically turned to desert could be brought back into production. In the USA alone, salt-rich soils account for £4 billion in lost agriculture per year.

Many crops are lost to poor soil or drought. Plants genetically modified to resist poor conditions may help some countries grow more food for their people.

Something for nothing?

Critics say that the GM technology used on these plants is like applying a sticking plaster to a complex problem. The plants pump the salt back into the soil, so the problem of soil quality remains. They argue that it is preferable to use better irrigation methods so that the high salt levels do not occur in the first place.

One of the advantages of modifying plants in this way is that no new genes are inserted, just more copies of existing genes. This gets round the problem of introducing new genetic material from animals or other plants. Time will tell what other effects this could have on the plant itself, or on its environment, but if successful, amplifying plants' genes could bring large areas of land back into production.

problem. Success stories certainly exist. At the beginning of this book, we looked at the story of cotton in India. A bacterial gene was put into cotton plants. This gene makes a chemical that kills bollworms. Bollworms normally eat and destroy cotton plants. But cotton plants containing the new gene killed any bollworms that ate the plants. The new cotton plant variety was called 'Bt'.

Planting GM cotton has increased yields by helping the plants resist attack from the damaging bollworm.

More tough choices

The genetic modification of plants and animals presents us with many difficult issues, such as whether we have a right to mix genes between species and what effect this will have on the environment.

Even if we are unsure about the case for GM crops in rich countries where food is plentiful, there is a much stronger argument for any technology that helps countries where food is scarce, conditions are much harder and chronic malnutrition and poverty are an ongoing enormous

Its supporters claim Bt allows farmers to use less pesticide. This makes it cheaper and more environmentally friendly because the chemical only kills moth and butterfly caterpillars. The makers say that it increases cotton yields by between 30 and 80 per cent.

Kiran Sharma is a scientist at the International Crops Research Institute for the Semi-Arid Tropics (ICRISAT) in Hyderabad, southern India. He says:

"People in the west (the rich countries) can protest

against us using GM all they like. They can afford not to use the technology. Here, we don't have the choice."

Suman Sahai is the organiser of an anti-GM group in New Delhi, India. She has studied 100 farming families growing GM and non-GM cotton. She has a different view:

"The (GM) companies have nothing to offer the poor. The public is completely excluded from any decision-making. Why gamble on a potentially dangerous technology with economic risks, when old fashioned selective breeding has served so well?"

Govindarajan Padmanaban is a biotechnologist at the Indian Institute of Science in Bangalore. He thinks the farmers know best:

"Farmers have bought it (Bt cotton) left and right. They are cleverer than the activists (protestors) or the companies. They won't buy things if they don't work."

Spanning the world

Cotton is not the only crop in developing countries to get the GM treatment. GM crops are currently grown on over 60 million hectares of land worldwide. That's about the same as the area of France. Countries include Argentina, China, South Africa, Colombia, Honduras, Mexico and Indonesia. Recent developments include a variety of rice that has been made to produce high levels of a chemical called beta-carotene. The human body uses beta-carotene to make vitamin A. If people do not have enough vitamin A, they go blind. This is a widespread problem in developing countries. It is hoped that the enriched rice will help prevent some of this blindness, but it is too early to say for certain whether it will help.

Another development involves a gene from the Amaranth, a South American plant used to make flour. A gene from the Amaranth has been inserted into potatoes. The gene increases the protein content of the potatoes by 30 per cent. Another good idea? It might appear so. But for every argument in favour of the technology, there is one against. Critics argue that it is better to concentrate on local crops with naturally higher protein content.

23

Could genetically modified rice help improve people's sight in developing countries?

GM companies; the answer or the problem?

Some people believe that the biotechnology companies have forced GM products onto poor farmers. The companies have invested a great deal of money in developing the technology and they need to get a return. Look back at the experience of GM soya in Argentina in the last chapter. The company that developed the resistant soya also manufactures the herbicide to which it is resistant. Farmers have to buy both products. The worry is that companies like this can control a large part of the agricultural market.

Some people believe that GM food threatens traditional ways of producing food, and damages local economies. They argue that the real cause of world hunger is not lack of food, but poverty – the lack of money to buy food or own land to produce and sell it. So, whilst some people believe that GM food will solve world hunger, others believe that it may create a bigger problem by concentrating power in the hands of big business.

The way ahead?

ICRISAT is a public-funded international agricultural research institute, funded by several governments and organisations. Its director general says:

"We see ourselves as the acceptable face of GM, since we are trying to ensure the products we are developing will benefit the poor in the semi-arid tropics. We only use GM when other more conventional means of improving crops are not available or do not work, and when we are sure of the safety of the GM crops. We have evidence that GM crops, such as Bt cotton, help improve the environment and the lives of the poor."

Perhaps we need to take the arguments both for and against GM technology seriously, and to recognise there is room for old and new technologies. One thing seems certain. It is up to the developing countries to be involved in the new technology and to decide for themselves.

Some people believe that GM technology will harm traditional ways of producing food. Others believe that GM technology can enhance people's lives.

From 'Pharming' to Fabrics

We have seen how bacteria can be modified to produce treatments such as insulin. Other genetically produced medicines are now used to treat lung clots, growth hormone deficiency and infertility. Plants can also be modified to produce drugs. Since medical drugs are also called pharmaceuticals, the cultivation of these new plants for the production of medicines has a new name – 'pharming'! New, non-medical products are also being made through genetic engineering. The revolution is gathering pace.

Scientists have manufactured artificial spider silk proteins in goat's milk, creating strands stronger than steel.

Help for haemophiliacs

Haemophilia is a disease in which the blood does not clot. If a blood vessel is damaged, a scab will not form and it will bleed for a very long time. Haemophiliacs lack a blood-clotting agent called Factor VIII. Factor VIII can be obtained from blood supplies but it is hard to ensure it is completely free from contamination by viruses. Genetic engineering allowed scientists to manufacture Factor VIII in the lab.

Stronger than steel

A biotechnology company in Canada is developing a way of producing artificial spider silk for use in making artificial tendons and ligaments. These are the structures that hold muscles onto bones and support the skeleton. In a complex process, silk-producing genes are taken from a spider and put into goats. Once in the goats, the spider genes produce silk proteins which can be collected in the goats' milk. The proteins can be turned into Bio Steel, a light fabric that is stronger than steel. The material can then be used to make the artificial tendons and ligaments.

In the future, when Bio Steel is fully developed, its uses will not be limited to medicine. Fishing lines, bullet-proof vests and new fabrics may also be created from Bio Steel.

Combating lung disease

In 1993, scientists created a genetically modified sheep which could supply medicine for treating people with a lung disease called emphysema. The sheep was called Tracey and she was genetically modified to contain human genes. The human genes meant that when she grew to adulthood, Tracey was able to make milk containing large quantities of a substance called human alpha-1-antitrypsin (AAT). This chemical is used to treat people suffering from emphysema. Tracey went on to have two lambs, one of which was also able to produce AAT in her milk. A thousand Traceys could satisfy the needs of every hospital in the world.

Sheep can be genetically modified to produce useful products, such as treatments for lung disease, in their milk.

GM gathers pace

The list of new products from genetically modified organisms (GMOs) is almost endless. Soon, there may even be 'designer' pets. Already it is possible in some countries to buy fish that glow in certain kinds of light. These products are not all for use in the medical world. They include enzymes used in

the production of detergents, food such as cheese and yoghurt, biodegradeable plastics from plants, and bacteria that can break down waste and pollution, such as oil spills.

The genetic revolution is gathering pace and could save or improve the health of many people. So why are some people concerned? Whilst many of the arguments against genetically modified food do not apply to drugs, problems of contamination can still arise. Maize that had been modified to produce a pharmaceutical protein was found growing in fields of normal soya beans. The company involved was ordered to pay around £2 million in clean-up costs.

In another case, a team of scientists in Arizona, USA, inserted virus genes that cause severe digestive problems into tomato plants. They hoped to use the illness-inducing plants to help them make a vaccine to the illness. To avoid contaminating or mixing these tomatoes with edible tomato plants, they are using a white tomato!

Scientist have put virus genes into white tomatoes.

26

GENE THERAPY

In 2003, another race finished, similar to the one that ended in understanding the structure of DNA in 1953. This time the goal was to discover the sequence of bases (the 'letters') that make up the human genome (the entire human genetic code). It was called the Human Genome Project. Knowledge of the human genome means that we may be able to fix faulty genes in humans – a process known as gene therapy.

This is the logo for the Human Genome Project.

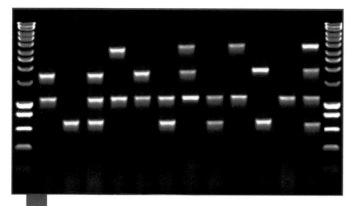
Scientists can analyse DNA samples to identify genes that cause disease.

Genome

The Human Genome Project was started in 1995. Unlike Watson and Crick's race, however, this project was about co-operation, rather than competition. It was also truly international, involving governments, medical charities, and pharmaceutical companies from all over the world. Because of improved techniques and increased computer power, the target date of 2005 was beaten. By the end of 1999, the genetic code for one complete human chromosome was known. By 2001, nearly 95 per cent of the genome for all of the

23 pairs of chromosomes in humans had been discovered and a kind of 'rough draft' produced.

Two years later, the goal was reached. Around 25,000 genes had been identified. These are made from over three billion bases. Perhaps surprisingly, it was found that only about three per cent of the three billion bases actually formed the genes themselves. The remaining bases of the DNA strands do not appear to be part of the genetic code at all. Scientists think that instead of forming the actual genes, the remaining bases may play an important role in controlling the genes. They have yet to find out what this role is and how it works.

The gene repair shop

Mapping the entire human genome was not just a piece of brilliant science. Understanding a gene means that we know the protein it creates. Knowing the protein gives us a good idea of what it does and how it affects the body. Therefore, in inherited diseases, we can now identify the faulty gene and, in the future, perhaps we will be able to cure genetic disease.

Gene therapy

Knowing about a faulty gene is not the same as fixing it, however. The path towards repairing faulty genes in humans – gene therapy – is a long and difficult one. We have already seen how genes can be removed and inserted into bacteria and even into plants and animals. But in humans, there are far greater risks and responsibilities. The price of failure is far higher – human beings damaged for life, and perhaps their children too if they inherit a faulty gene.

Plan of action

Earlier in the book, we were introduced to a condition called Severe Combined Immune Deficiency (SCID, see page 4), which requires sufferers to live their lives shielded from the outside world.

SCID is a rare genetic disorder, crippling a patient's immune system so that they cannot fight off infection. One way to save a SCID patient's life is with a bone marrow transplant. But to do this, the doctors have to find a donor who has the same bone marrow as the patient. Finding such a match is very difficult.

SCID is caused by a faulty gene. The gene is normally responsible for producing a protein – an enzyme called adenosine deaminase, or ADA. ADA is necessary for certain kinds of white blood cells, called T-cells, to function normally. In healthy people, T-cells recognise other cells in the body that have been infected by bacteria or viruses. The T-cells destroy the infected cells.

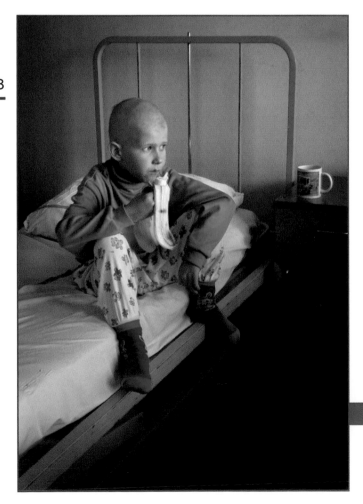

 ## How is gene therapy used to treat SCID?

To use gene therapy to treat the faulty T-cells in SCID sufferers, these steps are followed:

(1) Bone marrow cells are taken from the patient.
(2) A normal ADA gene from a healthy donor is inserted into a virus.
(3) The virus is used to transfer this ADA gene into the patient's bone marrow cells.
(4) The modified bone marrow cells are put back into the patient where they divide and produce normal, healthy T-cells. The result is a healthy immune system.

Sadly, gene therapy in SCID sufferers has caused cancer in some patients.

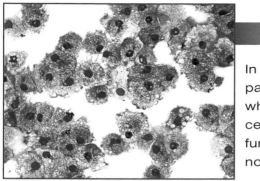

In SCID patients, the white blood cells do not function normally.

Although this sounds the ideal treatment and it has had some success, it has only been tried out on a small number of patients. In two other patients, complications arose and they developed a cancer called leukaemia, in which blood cells start multiplying out of control. It appeared that the virus used to deliver the gene had also activated another gene, which triggered the cancer.

Because of this problem, the gene therapy trials involving replacement of the faulty ADA gene were put on hold. The medical authorities thought it was just too risky to carry on until more was known about the possible damaging effects of the therapy.

'Fingers' to the rescue?

In April 2005, scientists in California, USA, announced they had developed another way of delivering the gene that did not involve viruses. They used a chemical 'finger'. The finger was made of the building blocks of proteins – amino acids – attached to a zinc atom. This chemical finger recognises exactly where the faulty gene lies, cuts open the DNA and allows the normal gene to be inserted. Because it is so accurate, the process does not appear to activate other genes that may cause cancer. It is not yet known how successful this new way of inserting a gene is, but it could be revolutionary.

Gene therapy promises cures for different genetic diseases, but it is too early to say how successful many of these treatments will be and how many lives will be saved.

29

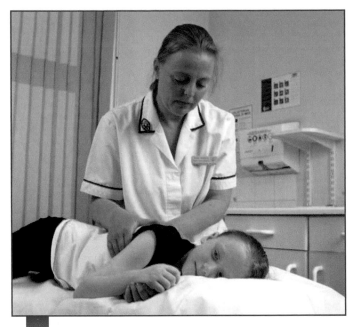

Cystic fibrosis patients must undergo regular physiotherapy to help them to breathe.

Cystic fibrosis

Whilst SCID is a rare disease, cystic fibrosis is a much more common genetic disorder. In the UK alone, 7,500 people suffer from the disease. In the USA, the figure is nearly ten times as high. In this disease, too much water is removed from the air passages and they become clogged with sticky mucus. This makes breathing difficult and means that the lungs are unable to remove bacteria and other harmful particles that collect there. Lung infections are more common in people with cystic fibrosis than in people with healthy lungs.

Gene therapy for cystic fibrosis

Like SCID, cystic fibrosis is caused by the absence of an enzyme, due to a faulty gene. Until recently, the only gene therapy treatment involved spraying the air passages with a genetically modified virus containing the normal gene. The process is difficult since the air passages are so narrow. In addition, the

treatment has to be repeated frequently and there is a danger that the body might see the virus as an invading organism, and could attack and kill it.

In December 2004, American scientists came up with a different approach to gene therapy for cystic fibrosis. They decided to use the patient's stem cells to deliver the gene.

Adult stem cells are made in the bone marrow. They are unspecialised cells. This means that they are able to develop into any other type of cell in the body, including the type of cells that line the air passages. Unlike the viruses that had been used to deliver the normal gene, stem cells are not attacked by the patient's immune system, since they came from the patient's own body.

Because the stem cells came from the patient's own body, they also carried the faulty gene. But the scientists replaced this with a normal gene. The stem cells were then made to develop into new lung cells. The hope is that the new lung cells

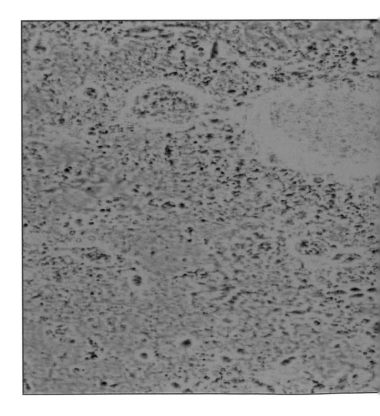

? What about the benefits?

The benefits of gene therapy could be enormous. Do we have the right to deny patients therapies that could cure previously incurable diseases or that can replace painful and unpleasant conventional treatments?

Would you be prepared to undergo gene therapy if you thought there was a good chance of success – despite the uncertainties? And who decides, anyway – the doctors, the patient, politicians, religious leaders or society as a whole?

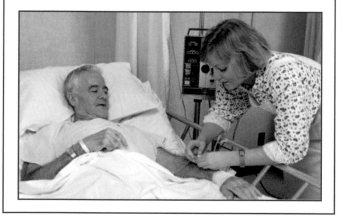

will work properly and not remove too much water from the air passages. When fully developed, this could provide a more permanent solution to a distressing and damaging disease.

Too far, too fast?

Like so much of the genetic revolution, gene therapy is a new and largely untested science. It raises many difficult issues. Many people are worried about the use of viruses to 'deliver' genes into cells. Although the viruses are altered so that they can no longer damage the inside of the body, what might happen if they mutated (changed their form) and became dangerous again? Often the viruses used come from animals. Suppose a virus that is relatively harmless in one organism becomes a killer in another? For example, it is now thought that the HIV virus that causes AIDS crossed from monkeys into humans, although this was not as a result of genetic modification. Whilst the virus did not harm the monkeys, it is lethal in humans. We have also seen that there may be other, unpredictable effects, such as the triggering of cancers. If one thing is clear, it is that genes do not often work on their own – they also affect other genes.

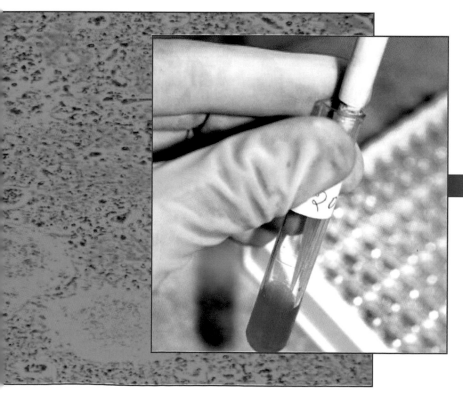

The left-hand image shows stem cells (the larger circles) as seen under a microscope. Stem cell gene therapy is a fast-moving area of medicine which may transform the lives of sufferers of genetic diseases.

Genetic Screening

Today, scientists are able to check embryos to find out whether they have any genetic abnormalities (faulty genes). This is called genetic screening. It can be used to tell whether an individual is likely to develop a genetic disease. For example, a rare genetic condition, called FAP, leads to life-threatening bowel cancer in later life. In November 2004, the UK's Human Fertilisation and Embryology Authority (HFEA) granted a licence to doctors to screen (examine) embryos for the gene that causes this disorder. If the gene was present, the embryo could be destroyed. If it was absent, the embryo would be implanted (see IVF box) and a healthy baby would hopefully result.

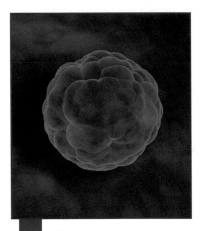

This is a blastocyst, a very early embryo in which the individual cells can still be distinguished.

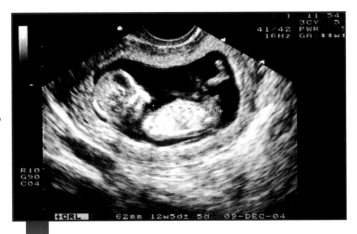

This is a scan of a 12-week-old foetus. Many of the features are already recognisable.

A difference of opinion

The HFEA was clear about its reasons for making this decision. They said:

"FAP is a serious condition – families with the genetic condition have a 50% chance of passing it on to their children, but using PGD (pre-implantation genetic diagnosis) can help these families have a healthy child."

However, a spokesperson for a group opposed to this kind of genetic engineering had a very different opinion. She said:

"We are not thinking about curing the disease, but about eliminating the carrier."

Discarding embryos with the faulty gene would mean that the gene could gradually be eliminated

What is IVF?

It is important to understand that much of the work described in these chapters involves IVF or 'in vitro fertilisation'. This means that eggs are fertilised outside the uterus or womb – in effect, in a test-tube. The early embryos, which are less than a few days old, can then have one or two cells removed for DNA analysis. Depending on the outcome, healthy embryos can be placed into the womb (implanted) for a normal pregnancy.

from the population. Many people think that this is a wonderful idea as it means that fewer and fewer people would suffer from the disease. But others think that the ability to get rid of a gene has other implications. They think that it means that we do not want people like this in our society, so we will prevent people with the gene from ever being born.

New science, old choices

The idea of genetic screening is not new. In the past, it was possible to look at several generations of families in which a genetic disorder occurred. From this it was possible to work out the likelihood of a couple having a child with a severe inherited disease, such as Huntington's disease. Such a couple would often be presented with an agonising decision about whether or not to go ahead and have children.

Now our understanding of the human genome has enabled doctors to screen people for genetic defects that might be passed on to their children. In the USA, many pregnant women and their partners undergo

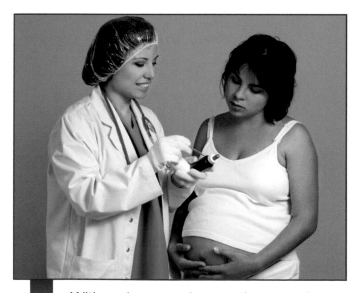

With an increase in genetic screening, more and more couples could face agonising decisions over the futures of their offspring.

DNA tests to see if the gene for cystic fibrosis is present. If both parents have one copy of the gene, there is a one in four chance their child will have the condition. Many then ask for a further test to see if the developing embryo actually has the condition. If this test is positive, they face the difficult choice of whether or not to finally end the pregnancy.

In addition, it is now known that the gene in cystic fibrosis is very complex. Sometimes the disease will occur, sometimes not. The outcome may depend on whether other mutations are present. Some pregnancies have been ended unnecessarily.

Decisions, decisions

The decision to discard an embryo is not taken lightly. A child might not thank its parents for allowing it to be being born with a serious physical handicap or a disease that would cut short its life. On the other hand, life is precious and many people, even those with severe handicaps (whether inherited or not), live full and productive lives. Few would not wish to have been born.

But there is a deeper issue. It concerns what we, as a society, consider to be acceptable in our fellow human beings. As genetic tests become more sophisticated, our ability to control the 'gene pool' (the total sum of genes within a population) will become greater. Even now, scientists are developing tests that will detect genes which increase the risk of breast cancer and a type of eye cancer called retinoblastoma.

There will come a point when we have to ask ourselves, as a society, where we draw the line. What about eliminating genes that may lead to lower than normal intelligence? What about genes that increase the risk of obesity? What do we eliminate and what do we allow through the genetic net?

33

Saving siblings

In April 2005, it was ruled that it was legal for a couple to screen and select embryos in order to produce a child who was a genetic match for an older brother. The brother had a severe blood disorder called beta-thalassaemia. In this disease, the sufferer's red blood cells are abnormal and he or she must be given blood transfusions regularly to stay alive. Stem cells from the bone marrow of the younger child could be given to the brother which would save his life. The stem cells would allow the older brother to make his own healthy red blood cells.

Babies on demand?

Despite the fact that the baby would not be put at risk, and it could save a child's life, many people objected. They claimed it was wrong to 'design' babies, even if it was for the benefit of others. The question is – where to draw the line? What if embryos were screened, not for the benefit of sick siblings, but for the benefit of parents? For example, a couple with a number of sons might want to make sure they had a girl next time, or even a blonde girl. They might want a child with higher than average intelligence. Screening for some of these features, for example, gender (male or female), is already possible. It is permitted in certain cases where particular genetic diseases are linked to one or other sex. Other characteristics, for example, intelligence, are controlled by a large number of genes, and screening would be technically much more difficult.

Changing genes in eggs and sperm

In gene therapy, normal genes are inserted into cells to replace faulty ones. There is no way that these modified genes can be passed on. But scientists also have the ability to modify genes in the sex cells – the eggs and sperm. This is known as germ line gene therapy and is banned almost everywhere in the world.

It does not just involve modifying the genetic make-up of one human being. Eggs and sperm pass on their genes to the next generation. By screening and altering them, we would pass on these modifications to all future generations arising from that particular individual. No one knows if this will ever happen, but one advantage of the technology might be that no embryos would be discarded by medical professionals. Any inherited defects could be repaired before fertilisation takes place.

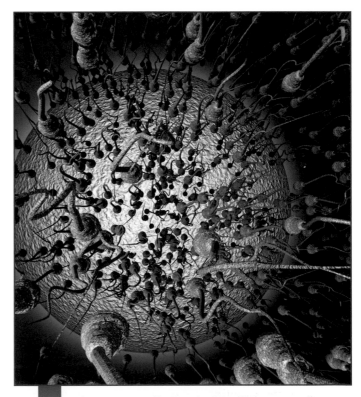

A sperm cell penetrates the egg cell during fertilisation to create an embryo. Genetically modifying eggs or sperm would mean that the new genes would be passed on to future generations.

CLONING AND STEM CELLS

Normally, an individual is created when two cells – a male sex cell and a female sex cell – join together. A clone is created from one ordinary cell – not a sex cell – and is genetically identical to its one and only parent. So cloning is the process of creating an identical copy of an original. Clones can be any organism – a bacterium, a plant or an animal. In May 2005, British scientists announced they had created a cloned human embryo for the first time in the UK.

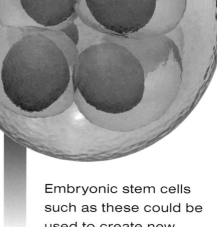

Embryonic stem cells such as these could be used to create new tissues to treat the person from whom the clone was obtained.

How was it done?

The cloned human embryo was produced by taking a donated human egg cell and removing its genetic material (the nucleus). A skin cell was then taken from the patient and the nucleus from this cell was injected into the donated egg cell. Under the right conditions, the egg cell began to divide, forming an early human embryo, from which stem cells could be extracted. This embryo was genetically identical to the patient as no other 'parent genes' were involved.

were failing. Since the cells would carry the patient's own genes, they would not be rejected by the body's immune system.

Stem cells from clones

The British scientists were jubilant at their success. The cloned embryos could act as a source of embryonic stem cells. Stem cells are 'master' cells that can develop into any tissue in the body. Since these stem cells came from embryos, they were far more 'flexible' than adult stem cells (see page 30). It meant that practically any cell or tissue, that was genetically identical to a patient, could be developed. These cells might be used to cure their own diseases or even build them new organs that

Identical twins are genetically the same, that is, they are clones of each other. They occur naturally but we could in theory produce clones of living people.

Benefits of stem cell therapy

Permanently curing diseases such as Parkinson's disease have now become possibilities. In this case, the stem cells from an embryo, cloned from the patient, might replace dead nerve cells in the brain. Such therapies are likely to be still a decade away, however. Cloned cells could also pave the way for the development of new drugs specially designed for individual patients. They would also allow the study of the diseases themselves.

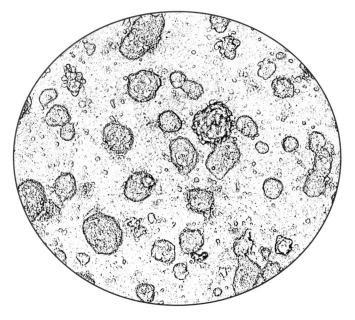

The pendulum swings

However, many people are appalled at the use of human embryos in this way. They feel that this is the first step to producing a fully developed cloned baby. Even if this did not happen, the protestors feel that the destruction of the embryos afterwards is similar to killing a person. Others feel that it is too early to develop these new techniques without knowing what the dangers might be. Since cloned cells are genetically identical, a single 'cell line' might introduce a harmful gene into hundreds or thousands of patients. The development and use of cloned human embryos to treat diseases raises difficult issues. It is important to understand what is involved. To do this, we must distinguish between therapeutic and reproductive cloning.

Therapeutic cloning

Therapeutic cloning involves developing cloned embryos so that their stem cells (above) can be removed and used in research or in developing gene therapy treatments. The embryos are not allowed to develop for more than a week and are then destroyed once the stem cells have been removed. They are not yet human beings in the real sense of the word, but many people believe that, since they have the ability to grow into human beings, they should be treated with the same respect. They believe that therapeutic cloning is unacceptable.

Reproductive cloning

Reproductive cloning would involve the cloning of a human being to produce a fully developed, genetically exact copy of that person. As far as we know, this has never been done. The ethical issues that would arise of dealing with 'failed' or damaged embryos or foetuses are almost unimaginable. Reproductive cloning is banned internationally.

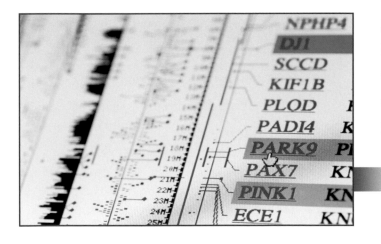

Embryonic stem cells may be able to replace the nerve cells that die as a result of Parkinson's disease.

THE FUTURE

Many new developments in genetic engineering are likely to be in the medical field. Research is being carried out into the possibility of finding cures or treatments for many dangerous or distressing conditions. For example, genetic treatments for some cases of blindness, deafness, hepatitis, cancer, brain diseases, Tourette's syndrome, heart attacks and strokes are currently being developed. In the future, could genetic engineering in the medical world help to prevent thousands or millions of deaths each year?

A healthy future?

In February 2005, scientists in Michigan, USA, announced they had used a form of gene therapy to cure deafness in guinea pigs. The research raised hopes that the same technique might work in people. Deafness often results from tiny 'hair cells' in the inner ear being damaged. This can happen after exposure to loud noise or certain antibiotic drugs, or simply from old age. In embryos, there is a gene that controls the development of inner ear hair cells. Scientists extracted this gene and put it into the inner ears of the guinea pigs. It helped to generate new hair cells and restore hearing by up to 80 per cent.

Would this work in humans? It is possible, but it is some way in the future, by as much as ten years. In addition, the scientists used a virus to get the gene into the guinea pigs' ears. There is a possibility that the virus could be attacked and killed by the human immune system, which would mean that the gene would also be destroyed. Future research may show if it is possible to use stem cells to deliver the gene.

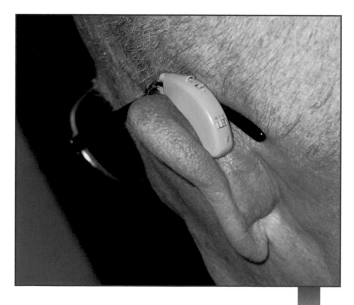

In the future, gene therapy may be able to cure some forms of deafness.

More GM treatments

Scientists are exploring the possibility of using adult stem cells to tackle liver disease. They want to take stem cells from the patient's bone marrow and introduce them into the liver. It is hoped that the stem cells will start to behave like liver cells and help the liver repair itself.

In the future it may be possible to treat infectious diseases like tuberculosis (TB) with vaccines that are made of genetically engineered DNA. TB is caused by a bacterium. A segment of DNA could be modified so that it contains genes from the bacterium. However, the DNA would not cause the disease to develop in humans. The idea is that when the DNA is injected into humans, the individual will build up antibodies against the bacterium genes. Then, if they are ever exposed to the actual TB-causing bacteria, they will be immune. This may be more effective than traditional vaccines.

Will the children of the future have 47 chromosomes instead of 46?

A new treatment for AIDS?

Perhaps the most important development of all would be to use genetic modification to find new treatments for AIDS. AIDS is caused by a virus called HIV. AIDS is widespread in many parts of the world and although modern drugs can be effective in slowing down the disease, it is still often fatal. In some African countries, over a quarter of the population is infected with the virus.

Scientists know that rhesus monkeys are resistant to HIV infection. They have a gene that codes for a protein that attacks the HIV virus. Humans have a different version of the same gene, but it does not protect against HIV. Scientists think that they may be able to genetically modify the human version of the gene so that it produces the killer protein. This may create a cure for AIDS.

More and more

Now there are even plans to 'build' artificial chromosomes as a way of delivering many different genes at the same time. Modified viruses, the normal method of inserting new genetic material, can only deliver short lengths of DNA – a few genes at most. Soon 'multiple genes', up to 1.5 million bases long, may be added to artificial chromosomes. If it ever happens, some scientists see artificial chromosomes as the most promising method of gene therapy. Maybe children in the future will not have the usual 46 chromosomes; perhaps instead they will have 47!

Eugenics: the final solution?

Eugenics is the deliberate attempt to change or modify populations. In the 1930s and early 1940s, the Nazis attempted to exterminate entire groups of people, including Jews, gypsies and handicapped people. Their goal was to produce a pure or 'master' race that would eventually dominate the world. Their method was not gene modification, but the systematic extermination of over seven million people.

Throughout history, societies have tried to rid themselves of groups who were different from themselves, often on religious or racial (ethnic) grounds. In more recent times, this has become known

In the future, gene therapy may be used to enhance sporting ability and build muscle.

improve sporting performance is a big problem. Soon, it may be possible to use gene therapy to make muscles respond better to exercise. The research is aimed at developing treatments for muscular dystrophy. But there is a more sinister side. The head of the research team says this:

"Half of the emails I get are from patients. And the other half are from athletes."

Designer world?

In the book 'Brave New World', Aldous Huxley describes a world where human beings are created by genetic engineering. Each person fulfils a certain role in society and does a certain job. There is no disease or disability, and everyone is very happy – or, at least, feels they are. We all want better societies. None of us likes problems, such as hunger or disease, that are so common in our world today. But we have to ask ourselves what price we are prepared to pay for the better world we want. For example, the use of drugs to

Rights or wrongs?

The guinea pigs used in the experiment at the start of this chapter were first deafened by means of antibiotics. Many people would feel concern about the treatment of animals in this way. However, almost all medical genetic work first involves work on animals. It would be unacceptable to apply the treatments directly to humans. It is also true that some of the early promise of genetic engineering has not yet been fulfilled. There has been some success, but also some setbacks and failures. As with much of the genetic revolution, it is not yet clear how wide-ranging or dramatic the benefits will be.

39

as 'ethnic cleansing'. Ethnic cleansing is a kind of eugenics. Eugenics may not always be as evil as the examples given. Some people (including Francis Crick, who discovered the structure of DNA) believe it is our duty to use modern technology to change and 'improve' populations by eradicating not individuals or groups, but faulty genes. Others think history has taught us to beware of these ideas.

In 1994 in Rwanda, ethnic cleansing killed between 500,000 and one million people. The people in refugee camps such as this were the lucky ones who escaped with their lives. Could genetic engineering lead to a new kind of ethnic cleansing?

THE DEBATE

The following is part of a recent public debate among four people about our ability to genetically screen or modify embryos in order to eliminate unwanted features or introduce new ones. The debate was called, 'The Search for Perfection'.

The debates surrounding genetic engineering are wide-ranging and should involve every one of us.

John is a supporter of gene therapy and the modification of humans.

He says: "To choose to bring a child with diseases or disabilities into this world is morally a problem. A child born permanently deaf, or lame, or blind, or with a short life expectancy would not be happy if these features were deliberately chosen. Why, then, do some people feel that designing children to be healthy, talented or to have some other beneficial feature might be wrong?

If it's not wrong for a parent to wish to have a bonny, bouncing baby boy, how does it become wrong if we have the technology to grant our wish? If creating a world with less disability and disease seems preferable, then, like me, you will believe in reducing disability and disease and increasing health and good fortune."

Tom has achondroplasia, which is an inherited disability causing restricted growth.

He says: "It's always entertaining to listen to John. Perhaps less so this time because the world he has in mind wouldn't have me in it. Or my two kids, or my dad. We cannot approach the dilemmas and choices John talks about in isolation. The world is messy and complicated, as are many of the things we do to intervene (bring about change), like surgery, genetic screening and Prozac (an antidepressant drug). They seldom do exactly what they are meant to.

One result of our many interventions is a reduced tolerance of diversity (difference). Because we can now screen pregnancies for certain genetic conditions, there's also a reduced tolerance of disability. We are entering a world where we can intervene in the genetic lottery. The 'eliminate at all costs' mentality is a real problem. Disability encourages interesting and creative ways of looking at the world. And a good society looks after its weakest members regardless of disability or disease."

40

Kathy is an editor of a fashion magazine.

She says: "Unlike Tom, you could say I don't live in the real world. But like it or not, cosmetic enhancement (improvement) is part of the real world and there will always be a demand for these procedures. If people believe a nose job will transform their lives, it is not all down to magazines like mine; it's because they are looking for self-respect and confidence in an increasingly dog-eat-dog world.

As soon as the geneticists can tweak an embryo to produce a blonde, blue-eyed, long-limbed baby, there will be a customer. But the future population of Barbie dolls won't necessarily be content. In my experience, perfection often leads to more insecurity – and ultimately more surgery."

Donald is a religious leader.

He says: "We recently had a family in the USA who were allowed to use IVF to choose an embryo of the same sex and as close a match as possible to their child who was suffering from a serious bone

marrow disease. That same week, in another country, a family was turned down when they asked for IVF to select a girl to replace their only daughter lost in an accident. They claimed it was their right to re-establish the gender balance in their family.

For all the anguish of that second individual case, we are all part of a wider society. There really is a difference between the medical and non-medical situation. You should not make your own preference a factor in the desirability of a child. The dream of perfection is an illusion. It's who we are inside that matters. Is genetic engineering going to bring peace to the world? I don't think so."

Each of the four people in our debate has a different viewpoint. Who would you agree with and who do you think is wrong?

Would you really want to live in a society where everyone is 'model perfect'?

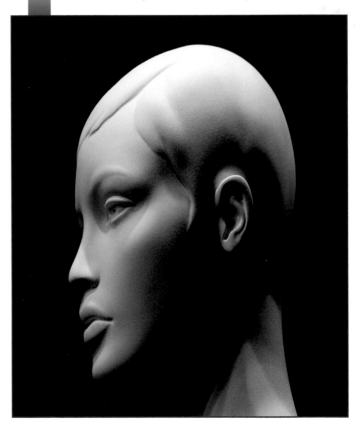

The search for perfection

The debate highlights some complicated issues and choices. If we have children, most of us would want them to be healthy, strong and happy. But is that the same as being free from all medical conditions that we might see as disabilities? Is it acceptable to deliberately select a future child so that they can be used to help an otherwise incurably sick brother or sister?

Of course, as we have seen, the genetic revolution goes far beyond our ability to intervene in our own development. In theory, we can change the genetic make-up of any organism we choose, from a bacterium to a plant to a human. Perhaps there are really only two issues we need to consider. The first is why we want to intervene in this process; the second is what are the likely consequences?

The why question

The 'why' question will vary for different individuals, just as it did for the people involved in the debate about perfection. The answer will reflect our own values and background. What we think is acceptable will not be acceptable to other people, just as what they think is OK may not be acceptable to us. We should respect those differences. There may be some ideas, however, that most societies would utterly reject. These are ideas to do with trying to change or even eliminate whole groups within society, on the grounds that other members of the society find them unacceptable. We are still a long way from such developments, however.

The what question

The 'what' question is, in some ways, even more difficult. We cannot easily predict the consequences of

our actions, particularly in the long term. Remember Tom's argument when he says,

"We cannot approach (these) dilemmas and choices in isolation. The world is messy and complicated."

When we change something, other things change as a result. We have seen evidence for this throughout this book. We can still try, however, to use our best science to predict what the outcomes may be. The whole of human development has included an element of risk, and our move into the genetic age is no exception.

To know or not to know?

Let us return to genetic screening. A genetic disease called haemochromatosis is caused by the build-up of iron in the body. This leads to liver damage and heart problems. It can be treated by removing blood from the patient regularly. A medical team in Australia offered to screen nearly 12,000 people for the condition. They obtained an agreement from medical insurers that people who tested positive would not be charged higher premiums (rates) for their medical insurance, since those affected would be offered treatment.

The tests were accepted by 96 per cent of those offered it! Of the 47 individuals who were identified as having the genetic defect, all but one began treatment. The study was a success.

But not all conditions are this straightforward. Tests for certain kinds of cancer only give an idea of the likelihood of contracting the disease – they do not give a yes or no answer. Knowledge of this risk could worry people, as well as helping them. Although the insurance companies were sympathetic in the Australian case, there is no guarantee they would be this understanding in all situations.

Once again, we are faced with the difficult question of where to draw the line. Would we want to know if we had a potentially fatal disease – an early warning could save lives, but it could also cause a lifetime of worry. Would we want our families to know? Might we eventually create a new 'class' of people with known genetic conditions who are discriminated against by employers, or insurers, or other members of the community? Could we be creating our own 'brave new world'?

Shouldn't we all believe that every human is wonderfully unique, and embrace the differences in our society? Or should we use our scientific knowledge to eliminate all genetic disease?

No going back

It could be argued there is no going back. We cannot 'unmake' the technology, but would we really want to, even if we could? The genetic revolution brings with it great responsibilities. How we approach them may be critical to our very future.

43

CHRONOLOGY

6000 BC – Sumarians make beer and wine by using a micro-organism, yeast.

2500 BC – Farmers in Egypt save seeds from plants producing the best crops in order to plant them the next year. This is an early example of selective breeding.

1719 – A London gardener, Mr Fairchild, creates Europe's first hybrid plant by crossing two flowers, a sweet-william and a carnation.

1865 – Gregor Mendel, an Austrian monk, shows that characteristics in pea plants, such as height and flower colour, are passed from one generation to the next in distinct 'units'. Previously, it was thought that characteristics from parents (such as short and tall) blended together in their offspring, producing, for example, a medium height individual. These units are later named 'genes'.

1869 – Frederick Miescher isolates DNA from cells for the first time, although its significance in inheritance is not yet understood: he calls it nuclein.

1902 – Chromosomes are identified as the means by which characteristics are inherited.

1902 – A British doctor, Archibald Garrod, observes that the disease alkaptonuria is passed on according to Mendel's predictions for inherited characteristics; it is therefore identified as one of the first genetic (inherited) diseases.

1909 – Wilhelm Johannsen uses the word 'gene' for the first time to describe Mendel's 'unit' of inheritance.

1911 – Thomas Hunt Morgan studies fruit fly chromosomes and shows that chromosomes carry genes.

1941 – George Beadle and Edward Tatum conduct experiments to show that genes work by directing the formation of a particular enzyme (a protein); this is known as the 'one gene, one enzyme hypothesis'.

1943 – William Astbury obtains the first x-ray diffraction pattern of DNA; this reveals that DNA must have a regular, repeating structure.

1952 – Alfred Hershey and Martha Chase show that only the DNA of a virus needs to enter a bacterium to infect it, providing strong evidence for the idea that genes are made of DNA.

1953 – Francis Crick and James Watson describe the double spiral (double helix) structure of DNA which allows the genetic code to be explained: they receive the Nobel Prize for their discovery in 1962.

1955 – Joe Hin Tjio describes the exact number of chromosomes in human cells as 46.

1959 – Jerome Lejeune discovers that Down's Syndrome is caused by an extra copy of chromosome number 21 being present.

1961 – Sydney Brenner, François Jacob and Matthew Meselson discover how the information making up the genetic code is transmitted to the protein-making machinery in the cell.

1968 – Scientists identify the enzymes that recognise and remove specific sequences of DNA, allowing genes to be 'cut out' of chromosomes.

1972 – Scientists produce recombinant DNA by joining DNA from different species and inserting this into a 'host' cell (a bacterium).

1973 – The first animal gene is cloned by joining a frog gene to bacterial DNA. The recombinant DNA is then placed back into a bacterial cell, which then reproduces.

1976 – The first genetic engineering (biotechnology) company, Genentech, is started; six years later it markets the first recombinant DNA drug, insulin.

1987 – Scientists discover that artificial chromosomes made from yeast can carry large fragments of human DNA.

1990 – The Human Genome Project is launched to map the entire sequence of human DNA: it is planned to take 15 years.

1994 – The US Food and Drug Administration approves the sale of the first genetically modified food, a tomato that lasts longer on the shelf.

1995 – Protection under the Americans with Disabilities Act is extended to cover discrimination based on genetic information.

1996 – A complete gene map of the lab mouse is

produced; it is found that it shares 85 per cent of its genes with human beings.

2003 – The Human Genome Project is completed, two years ahead of schedule; it is thought to be 99.99 per cent accurate.

2005 – British scientists successfully clone human embryos as a possible source of gene therapy and other treatments.

2005 – Britain's House of Lords rules that it is legal for a couple to screen embryos in order to select a match for an older child with a genetic disease: this means that stem cells from the second child can be used to treat the disease.

2005-2006 – Denmark becomes the first European country to tax farmers who want to grow GM crops. The money will be used to compensate other farmers whose crops may be contaminated by GM seed or pollen.

Council for Responsible Genetics
5 Upland Road
Suite 3 Cambridge
MA 02140
USA
Tel: +1 617 868 0870
Fax: +1 617 491 5344
Email: crg@gene-watch.org
Website: www.gene-watch.org
The Council for Responsible
Genetics monitors and encourages
debate about the social, ethical and
environmental implications of
biotechnology.

DEFRA (Department for
Environment, Food & Rural Affairs)
Information Resource Centre
Lower Ground Floor
Ergon House
c/o Nobel House
17 Smith Square
London
SW1P 3JR
UK
Tel: 08459 33 55 77
Fax: +44 (0) 20 7238 6609
Email: helpline@defra.gsi.gov.uk
Website: www.defra.gov.uk
DEFRA sets out the UK
government's position on GM food
and provides the results of field trials
and public consulations.

Food Standards Agency
Tel: +44 (0) 20 7276 8568

Email: adekunle.adeoye@
foodstandards.gsi.gov.uk
Website: www.food.gov.uk
The Food Standards Agency's
website provides information on
the latest developments in GM food.
The Food Standards Agency is a
food safety 'watchdog'.

GeneWatch UK
The Mill House
Manchester Road
Tideswell
Buxton
Derbyshire
SK17 8LN
UK
Tel: +44 (0) 1298 871898
Fax: +44 (0) 1298 972531
Email: mail@genewatch.org
Website: www.genewatch.org
GeneWatch monitors developments
in genetic engineering, particularly in
the medical field and human
genetics. It produces information and
'briefings' on topical genetic issues.

Monsanto
Monsanto UK Ltd
The Maris Centre
45 Hauxton Road
Trumpington
Cambridge
CB2 2LQ
UK
Tel: +44 (0) 1223 849 200

Fax: +44 (0) 1223 845 514
Website: www.monsanto.co.uk
Monsanto is one of the major
biotechnology companies. The
Monsanto website gives the
'industry' viewpoint, particularly in
relation to GM foods.

Soil Association
Bristol House
40-56 Victoria Street
Bristol
BS1 6BY
UK
Tel: +44 (0) 117 314 5000
Fax: +44 (0) 117 314 5001
Email: info@soilassociation.org
Website: www.soilassociation.org
The Soil Association campaigns for
organic food and farming (organic
farming means that no chemical
treatments, for example, pesticides or
artificial fertiliser, are used; genetic
modification is also not allowed).

Biotechnology Australia
GPO Box 9839
Canberra ACT
Australia 2601
Tel: 1800 631 276 (within Australia)
Fax: +61 3 9348 2934
Email: gtis-australia@unimelb.edu.au
Website: www.biotechnology.gov.au
Biotechnology Australia provide
factual information on biotechnology
to the Australian community.

Clone – Any living organism, from a single cell to a sheep (or human), that is genetically identical to another organism; identical twins are naturally occurring clones.

Cloning – The process of producing a genetically identical copy of another cell or organism. A number of different animals have been cloned. Although human embryos have been cloned for therapeutic purposes and research (see gene therapy), a fully developed human clone has never been produced artificially.

Embryo – An egg which has been fertilised and is beginning to develop by dividing into new cells. Even if only a small number of cells are involved, some people believe it has the same 'rights' as a foetus or even a fully developed human.

Foetus – An embryo that is developing in the womb and beginning to acquire characteristics that make it recognisable as a living being.

Gene – A short length of DNA on a chromosome that instructs the cell to produce a particular protein. The protein will then determine a particular feature such as eye colour or whether or not a person will suffer from an inherited disease.

Genetic modification (GM) – The introduction of new genetic material into an organism or cell, usually by means of a 'vector' such as a plasmid (bacterial DNA) or a virus.

Genetic screening or testing – Examining adults, foetuses or embryos for genetic defects or 'attributes'.

Gene therapy – Introducing 'normal' genes into an animal or human being in an attempt to replace faulty versions of that gene: in this way it may be possible to cure or treat certain inherited diseases.

Genome – The sequence of 'bases' on DNA making up the entire genetic code of a particular organism. Once known, the occurrence of particular sequences (or genes) can be linked to particular diseases or other features.

Inheritance – How particular features, such as height, eye colour and certain diseases, are passed on from one generation to the next.

IVF (In Vitro Fertilisation) – Fertilisation of eggs outside the womb. This is commonly used where couples have difficulties conceiving in the normal way or, more recently, where there is a risk of genetic disease. It is therefore now possible to 'screen' the embryos and only implant (replace) those that are 'normal' or have certain desirable characteristics.

Recombinant DNA – DNA that has been genetically modified, for example, by inserting a gene from another organism.

Reproductive cloning – Producing cloned embryos in order that a genetically exact copy of another organism results. So far this has not been carried out on humans and is currently banned in most countries.

Resistance – Ways in which an organism, such as an insect pest or bacterium, gradually builds up defences against a particular drug, chemical or other treatment.

Selective breeding – Improving a required feature, such as milk yield or resistance to disease, by only breeding with animals or plants with that particular feature, usually over many generations.

Stem cells – 'Undifferentiated' cells that have not yet developed into a particular kind of tissue, such as lung or nervous tissue. They may therefore be useful in replacing faulty cells or tissues. Adult stem cells are produced in the bone marrow; embryonic stem cells are cells taken from a very early embryo. They are more 'flexible' than adult stem cells and so may be more useful in gene therapy and research. However, they raise difficult issues about the possible use of embryos in this kind of treatment.

Therapeutic cloning – Producing cloned embryos in order that stem cells can be extracted and used for gene therapy and other purposes (see also 'reproductive cloning').

47

INDEX

48